George & Mildred

THE SONG OF SONGS

BY

Nicola Elliott

First published in 2023 by: Nicola Elliott

Dedicated to my Best Friend

MAUDE MILLAR
1927-2021
Forever In My Heart

Introduction

Welcome to a love story like no other.

A robin touches our hearts like no other bird does. A bird that wears its heart on its chest. It is a song that brings these two lovers together in this witty, educational, photographically-illustrated, heart-warming story. It tells of the adventures and challenges our beloved robins face in surviving and bringing up their wains the ‘robin way’.

It was spring and there was much excitement. It came with the promise of love and new life. All around there was a playfulness stirring as all of nature awakened to the change of season. The birds were flitting from branch to branch singing out their sweet melody. The grass was greener, the trees fuller and the insects were all abuzz among the beauty and sweet aromas of the flowering blossoms. While some animals awakened from their winter sleep, others gave birth. All of nature was rejoicing, singing with one voice in the celebration of new life.

This story begins at such a time as this. It begins in the townland of Blackhill in the Kingdom of Fermanagh. It was turf land where some nearby villagers had made their homes. At the very top of the hill there was one very special resident, a wee man called George. George was a robin.

George had spent much of the winter alone, but now it was spring and he had a new spring in his step. He was a man on a mission. He was out looking for the woman of his dreams. He was longing to find his true love and to start a family of his own, but the lassies weren't exactly lining up to get their feathery wings on him. George was a loner. Wintertime always made him grumpy and very antisocial. He spent much of his time chasing off any other robins that would come around the place. It was his land, his turf, and he intended to keep

WELCOME

things that way. However, somewhere deep down inside he knew it was time for change. Finding a good-looking woman would be no easy task. They were out there alright, but there were not many and he knew the competition would be fierce because he was not the only one on a mission to find true love.

George had another problem; he was a Mister Scruffy. No matter how he tried he always had feathers sticking up or hanging loose. Quite often he looked as if he'd been pulled through a hedge backwards, not a good look for a robin. Truth be told, he really didn't care how he looked. He was the 'take me or leave me' sort. Not exactly the right attitude to have when looking for the woman of your dreams. That being said he was happy in himself and that was all that mattered to him. George had a fighting chance, for he had an ace up his feathers, a gift he inherited from his mum, he was an exceptionally good singer.

His mum loved to sing and taught him many of her songs that had been passed down from one generation to the next over the centuries. She passed on that same passion to him. Singing came very naturally to him. He often sat high up in the treetops, watching over his territory, singing his little heart out. He often recalled a story his mum taught him about a very famous song writer called Solomon. He was a great king who wrote 1005 songs.

When God looked through his collection of songs, he chose only one and called it the 'Song of Songs'. George's mum told him it was a story of love. The song tells the story of a beautiful young woman who falls in love with a handsome shepherd. The young woman is working in a vineyard when their paths cross and it's love at first sight. However, she soon learns he is no shepherd but the king. George loved that story. He didn't have 1005 songs, but he knew it would only take the one, that 'song of songs' to win the heart of the one who would be his true love. He was on a mission, a quest from which there was no turning back.

Whether he was a Mister Grumpy or a Mister Scruffy, George would sing his songs loud and clear from the treetops. Every day he sat up on his favourite perch, ever watchful and listening for a reply to his song, even for a glimpse of a little lady that might pass by. Day after day, hour after hour he sang. Each morning as the sun would rise, he had a renewed hope that this would be his lucky day. Sometimes he would even forget to eat, but he knew a steady supply of porridge oats was always on the menu at the House of Millar. The loving and gracious lady of the house was not as well as she once was, but was cared for by her best friend, who also looked after George, making sure the lad never went hungry. George had come to like her but kept his distance. Humans were always worth watching his father

had taught him. It was so far but no further, to stay safe. He did find that a little difficult because the Irish oats were far too tasty to miss out on. The girl had taken a great interest in him and endeavoured to take his photograph at every opportunity. He found that a bit confusing and scary at times but the rewards far outweighed any of his fears. He soon learned that if the girl was out in the garden taking pictures, there was sure to be a fresh supply just put out. When he spotted her, he was over in a flash, excited to see where and what she was focusing on, because that was where the oats and any other goodies would be. Although the oats made him thirsty, they were a nice change from the juicy worms that were plentiful in the turf land, especially when it rained. Some believe the rain causes the earthworms' burrows in the soil to get filled up with water causing oxygen levels to drop, so they come to the surface to breathe. However, the theory with the most evidence is that earthworms find it easier to move across wet soil to find food, new living quarters or their true love. The vibrations of the rain hitting the surface of the soil causes them to come out of their burrows to the surface. George was brought up on worms, the fatter the better. They were easy prey with his exceptionally good eyesight. He always found it very amusing to watch some of his bird neighbours tap dancing on the grass to lure the worms below to

EOS
80D

pop their heads up. He'd often amuse himself by humming the tune, 'Good Vibrations' while they boogied. His great-grandfather had been a fan of the Beach Boys band in his younger days, resulting in many choice tunes being passed down through the generations of this music-loving family. The worms, lacking any brains, never really caught onto these devious tactics and fell prey every time to these charmers.

The Kingdom of Fermanagh is one of the wettest in the land all year long. It was on a wet and dark spring day, that after singing his heart out in the treetops, he went and polished off several mouthfuls of oats, which made him very thirsty. He flew over to the bird bath by the garden rockery to enjoy a nice cool drink. He bent over to take a few sips when another reflection on the water startled him. He looked up and there she was. He could hardly breathe as his heart was beating that fast. He had never seen anything so perfect and beautiful. She looked intently into his eyes. George could barely tweet never mind sing. She had heard him singing day after day from his favourite perch. She loved the sound of his voice, but it was the one song he sang early every morning that impressed her the most. She could tell it was not in his nature to give up and she admired that. They both stood there looking deeply into each other's eyes for a few moments. As she looked at him it felt as if

she could see deep down into his soul. Her smile broadened and at that moment she turned and flew off, leaving George in a state of sudden panic that he could lose her. She was the most beautiful creature he had ever seen. He shook himself back into reality and flew after her. She was only teasing him, for she really didn't want him to know just yet that her heart was his. They flew in and out and around about the trees, enjoying the fun of seeking each other out. He sometimes stopped and hid in the bushes, causing her to turn around and seek him out. He was learning fast, playing her at her own game. This was their song and dance. As the days went by their hearts grew fonder and fonder for each other, strengthening a now unbreakable bond. He discovered her name was Mildred, which made him inwardly laugh when he thought about it. His mum many years ago used to perch outside the living room window of the House of Millar and watch a box 'thing' through the window. It was a popular TV comedy show in the UK, called 'George & Mildred'. What were the chances of him hooking up with a local girl called Mildred? It was meant to be, he thought to himself. Mildred was a babe, there was no doubt about that. She was young and beautiful and never ever had a feather out of place. She was perfection, at least to George. Her only downfall was, she knew it. She was obsessed with her looks, especially how her bum looked in her

feathers, which makes you wonder why she was so taken with a Mister Scruffy like George. She loved all the attention George gave her. He often arrived with tasty treats for her to enjoy, after all, he wanted her to know what a good provider he would be. She often caught him daydreaming high up on his vantage point in the conifer tree. She did her fair bit of daydreaming as well, not that she would admit it. It was as if nothing or no one else existed or mattered outside of themselves. It was a magical world full of enchantment.

They got to know each other's adorable habits, some more adorable than others, but each saw the beauty of their own uniqueness in them. George always felt insecure in himself, questioning his every move. He would look at Mildred and wonder if he was truly good enough for her. In those moments of self-doubt, he often found reassurance by even the slightest gesture - a loving glance, a playful flight of 'catch me if you can' or a meal shared. He had a bad habit of obsessing over the little things about himself, fearing one wrong move could drive her away. He was always overthinking things. Mildred, like a true wee diva, endeavoured to keep him on his toes, giving him less time to think about himself and more time to think about her. They felt giddy with excitement and anticipation for the future that was theirs. At dusk you could hear them sing a chorus or two. It signalled a winding down

and preparing to find a safe spot in which to sleep. They spent their nights together now, finding comfort and security in each other's presence. No robin worth their tweet slept in on a morning, no matter how grey. Well before sunrise they would join with all the other pre-dawn singers such as the blackbirds and thrushes. The wrens, warblers and woodpigeons were next to join the morning chorus followed by the tits, sparrows and finches when it was light enough for them to see. All that singing created a mighty appetite in the pair, so it was always off to the House of Millar for those tasty porridge oats. They both enjoyed the oats, but often the competition would be intense, with their feathered neighbours and unwelcome passers-by each wanting their share of the bounty.

One neighbour, a certain Mrs Busybody, the resident magpie, was an arch-enemy to many in the neighbourhood. She was a plump snooty bird who always stuck her beak in where it wasn't wanted. That magpie had trouble written all over her. George had a few run-ins with her when she dominated the porridge oats, but there was no budging her. She was a messy eater, with food flying everywhere and her expecting everyone else to clean up after her. She was a true local of the Blackhills. Her family had lived there for generations. She was a ripe old age but never let herself go, always well dressed in her black and white feathers with

their attractive iridescent sheen that came to life in the bright sunshine. There had been many admirers over the years resulting in quite a large extended family who had all flown off to make a name for themselves, probably as gangsters in the criminal world. She was no birdbrain. Many believed she was the unholy godmother of the family, the criminal mastermind behind all the activities of the local cartel. She was rumoured to be a bit of a kleptomaniac, if you could believe the gossip. Seemly it ran in the family. The lesson here is, don't judge a bird by its outward appearance because there could be a kleptomaniac in there. Some would say magpies are not thieves, merely inquisitive, but you can’t believe all you hear. It's one of those conditions that gets worse with spring when nesting is taking place. Her whole family were famous for collecting all kinds of objects, particularly anything shiny, to decorate the nest. All the songbirds watched her like a hawk during spring, not because of the kleptomania but because of the many stories of eggs stolen and chicks kidnapped from their nests by the Magpie family. Mr and Mrs Sparrow had their nest raided last spring. They had nested in creepers covering the stable walls behind the House of Millar. A lovely inseparable couple. Like every female sparrow it was the size of his black chest bib that won her over. He did indeed have a very impressive black bib, thus

making him the man for her. She laid four eggs that spring. In all things equal they both took turns to incubate the eggs until hatching about 11-14 days later. Their nest was the talk of Bird Town, with the wonderful array of pigeon feathers used to line it. It was a comfy colourful home for the chicks. Several locals had remarked how rough the pigeon couple looked, but being in the know I can tell you the poor craters were getting plucked in their sleep. As soon as they decided to have a wee nap in came the notoriously house-proud Mrs Sparrow. She would stealthily sneak up behind them in a snatch-and-grab operation to pluck a feather or two if she could get away with it and off she'd scarper back to her nest. She wanted those glossy greenish and reddish-purple iridescent ones for her interior design project. Sadly, however, not all four of her chicks survived to fledge.

It was a fateful spring morning just after sunrise when an unspeakable tragedy took place. All four eggs had hatched with both parents busy to and fro from the nest to keep the wains as happy as possible. When Mum flew out, Dad would fly in and so it would go all day long, except this one day held an ominous unwelcome surprise. Mr Sparrow was having a good day, picking off some cabbage caterpillars in a neglected garden vegetable patch beside some derelict sheds down in the lowlands. It was outside his usual territory but worth the

the risk for this bounty. There were caterpillars everywhere and he was elated at the ease of these pickings, it just made feeding his family so much easier. He grabbed as many as he could manage on this one trip when suddenly, out of nowhere, a dark shadow fell over him and all he could see was an open drooling mouth of teeth coming straight for him. It was a wild black and white cat that roamed the area and who was only too happy to have a passer-by come for a visit. Mr Sparrow thought his time had come for sure when its front paws plunged right down in front of his beak. He dropped the caterpillars and flew straight up in the air between the cat's paws and in a backward flip with no room for error brushed past those sharp incisors. He felt one scrape across his back feathers as the cat leapt up in the air, paws outstretched. The warm breath of the cat filled the air around him as he dived under one of the cat's armpits, which it least expected, and made his escape. He flew up into a very high tree to catch his breath and check himself over. Everything was okay, apart from a missing back feather or two but nothing that would hold him back. That was a close call. He concluded it best to leave the caterpillars and the cat well alone in the future, as tempting as it was. Once he had gathered himself together, he headed back to the nest. As he got closer, he heard a very stressed and irate Mrs Sparrow. She was going mental around the area of

the nest. This was not good. His heart was beginning to pound in his chest because it could only mean one thing, an invader! He swiftly flew to her, she was breathless and distraught, but it was too late. A close relative of Mrs Busybody had raided the nest when he hadn't got back in his turn to feed the wains. He was in a state of disbelief. He couldn't get a word out of the missus, so he quickly checked the nest. He could barely bring himself to look, but one of his wee ones was gone. There were only a few fluffy feathers left sprinkled with blood. His heart sank in horror. He took some comfort in the fact the other three, although still frightened and on edge, were left unharmed. They both couldn't dwell on what had just happened for too long, with three lives still totally dependent on them. Thankfully, all three youngsters survived and grew up to have families of their own.

During spring, with so many now nesting, all the songbirds were on tippy-toes doing their best to keep their nests secret from any would-be raider. Mr and Mrs Sparrow were only one of many such tragedies, with some families being hit harder than others.

George had proven himself a good provider. He was flying about the stables at the back of the House of Millar when he noticed Mildred acting somewhat suspiciously behind the empty stable walls. She was carrying a beak full of moss in and out of the thick

briars and ivy that had become overgrown. She caught a glimpse of him watching her from an opposite fence post. She flew over to George, grinning from one end of her beak to the other. Her eyes were sparkling with life and excitement. It took a moment for the penny to drop. It was time! Well, he jumped straight up in the air in joy with her giggling at him. He couldn't stand still. He was a dithering mess. She turned and flew off, leaving him reeling. Once he realised she had flown off he calmed down a bit to take it all in, he was going to be a dad. In all the excitement he forgot to check out where exactly the nest was, but she was soon back with more moss. She showed him what was going to be home for the wains for the next four weeks or so. He loved the new setup. The nest was built inside an upturned wooden box, that nature was reclaiming around the back of the stable wall, well-hidden through the undergrowth. It was perfect, he loved it and her all the more for choosing it. People rarely came up to the disused stables. It was the perfect location for them to bring up the wains, especially with the porridge oats just over the hedge from them. It was a sensible and safe choice, unlike one of Mildred's very distant relatives, who had recently taken a liking to a man's bedroom. She'd flown in through an open window. The unmade bed looked cosy and still felt warm below her talons, so she wasted no time in starting to build

her nest in such a prime location. The man was downstairs having breakfast. Thankfully, the owner loved robins, he left her to it, undisturbed until the wains had fledged. Mildred, more level-headed in her choice, took full responsibility for building the nest as is the 'robin way'. George instinctively knew his sole purpose now.

He was to keep his woman well fed so she'd have all the energy she needed for the task and the egg laying that would be sure to sap her energy. He was flying about like a mad thing searching out the fattest and longest worms he could find, plus a few oats thrown in as well of course. Mildred barely stopped until bedtime. It was both exhausting and exciting for them both. Mildred wanted six babies, the most a robin can have in the one brood. George was not that keen to have so many because he knew the toll it would take on them both with so many beaks to fill. Four would do him nicely. Both of them cosied up together at night dreaming about those wide-open baby beaks begging desperately to be fed.

In three days, Mildred had the nest ready. Sometimes the nerves got the better of her and she'd have to take some time out, choosing to rest on the nearest hedgerow to the nest. She was on edge as this was going to be her first brood. Her emotions were all over the place. She was going to be a first-time mum, but the excitement and anticipation far outweighed

how scary it all was to her. She had an overwhelming sensation that life as she knew it was about to change forever. It was different for George, he had been a dad before, so he knew what was what and what to expect. He was nervous too. He had to keep alert and be extra vigilant against intruders or predators that could potentially threaten Mildred's life and the wains.

It was time for Mildred. She sat in the nest, discomforted and shaking as the first egg was laid that next morning. She was tearful, struck again with that overwhelming feeling that she was not going to be able to look after these teeny, tiny strangers who would need her so much. Then she felt panic, was it too late to shove it back inside where she'd know it would not get broken. The next thought flooding in was the realisation that she'd have to go through it all again the next morning and the next and next until all the eggs were laid. With the fifth egg laid came the inner sense that the brood was now complete. George barely had time to think, to take it all in, feeling somewhat overwhelmed himself. Mildred spent most of her time in the nest, turning and keeping the eggs warm and safe. She rarely took a break and even then for only ten minutes or so. The days seemed to melt one into another when on the thirteenth day she felt something stirring below her. She stood up carefully to look and sure enough little cracks were appearing on some of the slightly quivering shells.

She gasped in awe as her first wee one broke free into the world. By this time George was back with breakfast for her. She looked at him awestruck and he knew new life was breaking free. One by one each chick hatched its way out throughout the day. She removed each shell from the nest, eating a little for extra calcium to help fortify her for the challenges of parenthood. There were five naked wee bundles now totally dependent on them for food and warmth. Both of them were now responsible for keeping these jostling wee bundles happy and fed. It would be fourteen more days before these nestlings would be ready to leave the nest so Mum and Dad had an even more exhausting time ahead of them. Day after day they took turns in and out of the nest bringing all sorts of soft tasty morsels for them. With every day the nestlings grew bigger and stronger. There was great excitement when on the fifth day the chicks started to open their eyes, although it would be the eighth day before their eyes would fully open. Rows of feathers were appearing as well. They would be as good as covered by the tenth day. The flight feathers would be the last to develop, although after fledging from the nest it would be a few days before they would be able to actually fly. George and Mildred were so in awe when those little eyes started to open. The chicks jostled with each other in the nest for position and what a lot of screeching went on

when food arrived. There was a lot of pushing and shoving and craning of necks with wide-open orange mouths, each wanting to be fed there and then. They were too young for porridge oats at this stage. A robin chick can eat up to fourteen feet of worms whilst still in the nest, how's that for a gut-wrenching fact. Yuck! Each time a tasty morsel was devoured by the chicks they would present Mum or Dad with a cute wee bum stuck up in the air for them to take away their poop bag. Baby robins can't wear diapers, just in case you've ever wondered about that, but they do put their poop in a strong enough bag so the parents can carry it away. How handy is that! The really tummy-turning gross part, and I can barely bring myself to mention it, is that both parent robins for the first couple of days will eat many of these faecal sacs, yes eat, how gross is that? The chicks are too young to digest all the food they take in which makes them snack material for Mum and Dad. Once the poop starts having more bacteria, they stop eating them. George and Mildred kept the nest nice and clean and tidy as any respectable robin would, taking away the poop and dropping it well away from the nest. They were so tempted, for the fun of it, to use Mrs Busybody for target practice on the drop, but thought it best to leave her alone in case of reprisals. As you know, she's one bird you don't mess with. Mildred, being a first- time mum, was amazed how

quickly the chicks were growing up. In the early stages they looked like punk rockers, now they were feathered fluffy balls with two comical head tufts and were just about ready to leave the nest, which was now too small for them all. They just couldn't get comfortable, with each of them walking over each other to stretch those developing flight feathers. It was getting unbearable for them. Then the big moment arrived as one by one they jumped from the nest. The two very proud parents looked on, leaving them to find their feet in among the protective overgrowth. The fifth chick was not one bit happy about leaving and stayed put most of the day watching his siblings jump and scoot about below him in their new-found freedom. George did his best to encourage him out by calling to him and showing him food to entice him out, but not a move would he make. They gave up trying, the next move was up to the chick. The rest of the family had a ball exploring the area close to the nest in-between Mum and Dad feeding them. They always got all of a-flutter when food was on offer.

The weather was changeable as it always was in the Blackhills with nothing too exciting happening. Life was still buzzing all around with the air still full of anticipation and wonder as summer progressed. The fledglings were still exploring their strange surroundings in peace

and quiet on their first day out. They enjoyed the sunshine on their feathers, making them feel all warm and cosy. But suddenly, the sun's rays seemed to flicker above them, too erratic to be normal. The quiet was pierced with a screeching alarm call warning of danger overhead. The robin family all fled for cover in the overgrowth.

Instinctively, they knew to stay very still and very quiet. They waited, wondering what it was that struck such terror deep down into their very being. The fifth chick had nearly jumped out of what feathers he had. He promptly vacated the nest and hid down among the briars with the others. As they say, safety in numbers. Their wee hearts were all thumping in their chests, scared that even their breath would give them away. After what seemed like forever, George went back out into the open to check if the coast was clear. The sparrowhawk was gone. What a sigh of relief could be heard coming from them all. It was back to exploring.

Mildred flew over to George, relieved the danger had passed over. They looked into each other's eyes for a little while and he knew what she was trying to tell him. She had to leave, but it wasn't a farewell, more like I will see you soon again. She was a mum now and her instinct told her to go and build a new nest in preparation for a whole new set of wains

before the season for babies was over. She did have one very worrying concern. She was a mess, at least she felt she was a mess. She found an abandoned mirror on the rockery belonging to the girl and she was horrified to see how much weight she had put on. Her butt was huge, not to mention those stretch marks. She was traumatised at the sight, vowing not to go near those nice porridge oats ever again. She didn't realise she was looking into a 10x magnifying mirror, so it's no wonder she didn't look herself. Seeing yourself ten times bigger than you really are would be enough to put anyone stray in the head. She disappeared in a real flap. George watched her from the gate and was somewhat bewildered at her reaction and her speed of flight. He thought she was just perfect. He knew well enough how touchy she was about her appearance, being careful not to say the wrong thing at the wrong time.

His heart was sad at the thought of not having her about. He loved everything about her and to have her gone as he brought up the kids in the way of the robin was hard to bear. He would miss her terribly, but it was something she had to do. He couldn't get excited over the thought of another set of mouths to feed because of being so focused on getting this lot ready for the world they had just entered. Once she had recovered from her shock, Mildred flew back over to George. He nodded his head. She gently touched his beak with hers,

so torn between her love for him and her instinctual desire to nest. Even this short break from each other would feel like a forever farewell for them both but it would be only for a few weeks until they would catch up with each other again. She took a final look at the kids before she left. She loved them so much; they were a part of her but new life was calling her on. Away she flew, there was no looking back. George watched her fly over the bushes and through the trees until she was out of sight. He sighed deeply to himself and sighed again when he looked over at the five wains still totally dependent on him. He had sole responsibility for them now. He had to teach the robin way in all things for them to survive in this wonderful, curious world they had been born into.

They had just had their first lesson in survival against a possible overhead threat, now he busied himself teaching them how to fend for themselves, especially what was good and needful for their diet and wellbeing. A lot of what he did, they did pick up, so it was more about leading by example.

A few days after Mildred had left, they were out and about as usual watching Dad's every move and keen to each be the first to get to the food he brought. They still kept well hidden most of the time. This whole flying thing was still causing them too much bother, but

they weren't stressing over it as yet. It wasn't a great day weather wise, in fact, very much the usual for the Blackhills, cloudy with those occasional rain showers. Oh! What joy when the sun did manage to come out. Some of the fledglings decided to venture out a wee bit further to see what else was out there, exploring around the back of the stables. The long grass gave them some needed cover which was reassuring. Then, suddenly, out of the silence there was a swooping noise of wings. The fledglings heard their father's alert call, but it was too late. One of the wains was instantly grabbed in a set of sharp talons that weren't about to let it go. It screeched out in terror and then in pain as it was squeezed and held tight. Away, away up into the sky it was taken from its family to certain death. The sparrowhawk had been watching the family, waiting for the opportunity to snatch his prize away. George was furious and grief-stricken all at the same time. He reeled with rage around the stables, but what could he do? The truth was, absolutely nothing, the wee one was forever gone. The terrified fledglings had all taken cover among the briars and were safe but one of their number was now gone. They were shaking in fear from head to talon. George was distraught but he still had four mouths to feed, so he busied himself searching out food for them. The cries of his lost one would forever haunt him. What would Mildred think he wondered?

But she did know. She had seen nature's 'Top Gun' swoop into the Blackhills from her new nest site and knew exactly where it was heading. She carefully followed it, keeping under cover all the way, but by the time she got to the top of the hill it had already struck. There were no words for what she felt, she bowed her head and returned to her own task in hand. She wanted to be with George to console and help him through his pain as well, but nature's call was stronger within her now and she had to have the new nest ready.

The sparrowhawk was an awe-inspiring predator known to the locals as 'Top Gun' because of his speed and agility. There was no mercy at his talons if he got you in them. He had a bit of trouble with the ladies, not common knowledge and I'm certainly not one to be passing on gossip as you know. Now, from what I've heard he fancied a bird near the borders of the Kingdom of Fermanagh. She was 25% larger and twice as heavy as him, which actually is the norm for her kind, in case you're thinking he has a thing for the 'larger' lady. With the size difference she could easily whoop his behind if need be. In fact, this doll didn't take kindly to any of his advances. He courted her in the traditional way, but she wasn't having it. The more he tried to win her over the more annoyed she got. In the end, he gave up in fear for his life and high tailed it back to his home. That's a lot of rejection to cope with for

someone nicknamed Top Gun. Just so you know, if a female sparrowhawk decides the male courting her is not the man of her dreams and he fails to get the message, he could end up dead. Being a lady myself it gets you thinking! It's a good job our Top Gun got the message in time. He lives to love again, and unfortunately to kill again, to the dismay of the locals.

The day closed for a very grief-stricken robin. He couldn't bear to think what that evil-eyed sparrowhawk would do to his wain. He felt guilty but he could only do what he could do to protect them and accept that at times like this it would not be enough. The next few days passed without incident. The fledglings had developed their flight feathers which would help them evade any future potential dangers. They could all take to the trees and hide. They enjoyed flying and experimenting with all sorts of aerial acrobatics. They looked less comical now without their head tufts of fluff. Even their chests were darkening more and soon they would have robin-red breasts. In-between test flights they raided the cup of porridge oats. The competition between them for a beak full was fun to watch for the girl who was snapping away at their antics in the garden. The House of Millar was a safe haven for them. There was always a full cup of oats out on the garden rockery ready for those hungry beaks to get stuck in.

The girl was soon to learn of another contender for the oats, someone who came out in the dead of night. She was out in the kitchen one night reluctantly doing the washing-up when she noticed a wee rascal sitting on top of the Royal Albert Country Rose china cup set out for the robins. It was munching away merrily on the rim of the cup, having a feast of feasts. The girl was all excited to see it, running out with her camera to get a pic, which she just about managed to do. It was a wee woodmouse she called Stewart. The girl had so much fun with that mouse. It was the excitement of having some fur to photograph rather than something feathered that excited her. She invited him out for tea as well one evening. It was only the best for Stewart. A delicious slice of a jam and cream Swiss roll was carefully plated on a Royal Albert china side plate complete with the best napkin in the place in case any cream got on his long whiskers. The lady of the house had once told the girl that the quality of a place could be determined by the quality of the napkins used. Once she had placed the treat on the rockery, the girl sat waiting outside in the car for him to appear once it got dark. Sure enough, he was right on time and tucked straight into the piece of Swiss roll. To her surprise, he brought the family as well. She was thrilled to see them. The Swiss roll went down a treat and a lovely evening was had by all. The lady of the house was blissfully unaware that her very best china was being used for mouse and bird alike.

The girl reckoned it was best to keep that secret to herself. She never did tell her.

Stewart always came out as soon as it was pitch-dark. You would have rarely seen him or any of the family during the day. His first visit was always to the cup of oats. One occasion was nearly his last when the ghostly figure of a barn owl flew right over the cup. It was looking an easy meal as well but the girl's presence scared if off and it flew away in search of some other easier prey.

The robin fledglings were getting more and more adventurous with each new day. They had their wee quarrels but all was forgiven and life continued on as normal. The girl loved to see them about the garden.

One bright sunny morning she decided to take Teddy her dog out for a walk which didn't start so well. She walked around the side of the house with him only to be met with a very sad sight indeed. One of the fledglings had flown into one of the sitting room windows and had broken its neck on impact. Its body lay lifeless on the tarmac. It was so sad that such a thing should happen. She took the still warm body and buried it with honours among some beautiful orange garden flowers. Just with that George appeared on the boundary fence, he had just found out himself.

He was finding it all hard to take in because it was so close to freedom and its flight into adulthood. There was nothing he could do but mourn its death.

He flew back over to the others who were not too sure what was going on but again they realised another of their number was gone forever. As devastated as he was, he knew life for a robin was all about survival, especially through the winter months. He couldn't afford to dwell on his loss because his job was not yet done. He worked even harder to prepare them for adulthood and sure enough, one by one, they moved further and further away to find their own territories and live their own lives. One still lingered - there's always one! George would not feed him and pretty much ignored him altogether. It was time for him to leave home. They all had good singing voices so no worries there. It would soon be their time to sing their songs and sing that one 'song of songs' to win the heart of the true love he hoped they would each find. He watched each of them leave, there was no farewell or fond embrace because it was not the robins way. When the last fledge eventually got the message and left he sighed deeply with first grief and then relief. His job was done. It was now time to go find Mildred and see how the new nest was coming on. Just before he headed off, he flew down to the House of Millar to look for a mirror.

He reckoned the girl was maybe vainer than his Mildred, the cheek! He was relieved to see a mirror still sitting out on the rockery. He had a quick look at himself, giving himself quite a fright, I can relate! Well! It was a good job he did, for a Mr Scruffy he was. He couldn't believe his eyes. He couldn't let Mildred see him like this with all his feathers dishevelled and sticking up, she'd leave him for sure. His white feathers were a dull grey with dirt. He promptly headed for a nice clean puddle and gave himself a good once over. He checked his feathers and all was back in order apart from that one feather on his head that never wanted to lie down, but he knew Mildred found that a little endearing so he wasn't going to stress over it. There was nothing he could do with it anyway.

Mildred had briefly looked in on him and the kids a few times in the past, but had kept her distance. She saw only three wains. A wave of grief had washed over her then, but there was no time to dwell on it, because new lives were about to come to her and George once more. The whole cycle of life was about to begin again.

George had no trouble finding Mildred, he had sighted her on a few occasions. She waited for him high up on their favourite perch in the conifer tree. She sensed he was on his way.

They were elated to be back together again fluttering and flying about like mad things. She was in good shape having been on a slim-fast diet. It was natural foods the whole way for her now, resisting the call of those tasty fatty oats. They had fun playing 'catch me if you can' with a bit of 'hide and go seek' thrown in. It was bliss having no responsibilities and just each other once again. Soon enough it would be all about the wains again. George wasn't much good at games, but Mildred was and he had a fair job trying to find her. She had to help him out on a few occasions, else he would never have found her. He disappeared on her at one point. She went up onto a nearby shed roof to see if she could spot him. There he was, hiding among the miniature daffodils. She giggled in delight as she flew down towards him. He saw her coming. He was grinning from one side of his beak to the other as he quickly got some tasty goodies ready for her. She was impressed as always and enjoyed her wee treat. She smiled at him because it marked the beginning of a new family for them. They took some time out for themselves but nature drew them quickly back into its plan. Mildred soon felt that familiar unease in herself and knew it was time to lay the first of her eggs. She could not settle and felt so uncomfortable. She had been busy searching for and building a new nest. She showed George the new cup-shaped nest she had lovingly built. The new

abode was hidden high up in an ivy-concealed space between two large stones in the wall of a disused shed. The opening led to the inside of the shed. It was the only way in and out for them. The nest was situated on a wooden beam just below the corrugated roof. She had done a great job but George was a bit unsure about the choice of site. Anyway, he trusted her. Mildred positioned herself on the nest. She laid her first egg the very next morning.

She laid another three over the following three mornings until she knew that was that. Now, it was a matter of keeping the eggs warm and safe until they all hatched. George was busy as usual bringing food in and out to her until they hatched. All was going well for the couple, but all the toing and froing had attracted some unwanted attention... a pair of eyes was watching them very closely indeed.

One morning, George headed out as usual for more food for Mildred while she decided it was time to stretch her legs and have a poop of course. After all, what goes in must come out! She headed close by for a stretch and some fresh air, but it was an opportunity too good to miss for the dark, beady eyes that watched her. Before Mildred knew it,

Mrs Busybody the magpie flew in like a rocket and pushed her head down into the crevice where the nest was. She knew she had to be quick for Mildred was already screeching blue murder and dive bombing her from behind. George had heard her alert call and quickly joined her to distract the murderous magpie from the nest. Mrs Busybody reached as far as she possibly could down that dark crevice but it twisted around and she couldn't reach the eggs at all with her beak. She was too big and bulky to succeed. The noise around her was alarming and deafening which was distracting her from her mission. She reversed herself out, but not before getting a right good old peck on the butt from Mildred.

Mildred knew a bad ass when she saw one. The magpie flew off, enraged at her failure. She had five youngsters of her own to feed and a few eggs would have gone down a treat for them. Both robins settled themselves down, although they still felt somewhat irate with the ol' doll. George now understood why Mildred had chosen the nest site she did. The eggs were safe at least for now.

The big day came when the eggs started to hatch. One by one the wains hacked their way out of their shells. It was a lot of effort on their part but they made it, to the delight of Mum and Dad who got busy feeding those hungry mouths. The robin nestlings grew quickly over

the next two weeks. When the time was right and with lots of encouragement from their mum and dad, they left the nest to explore the wonders of the world around them. Mrs Busybody hadn't reappeared but was spotted nearby foraging for her own wains. She was not the only villain around the place. There was another prowling around the House of Millar. It was a lone feral cat, without owner or name. The fledglings were out exploring enjoying a nosy about in the gorgeous sunshine when their dad's frantic alarm call startled them. My goodness! What a fright they got. They were close to the nest, but all the chirping had attracted the cat's attention. The cat, a hunter by nature, was only following her instincts when she heard them.

She had crouched down among the overgrown grass and weeds to stay hidden. Little by little she advanced, stalking them from the field next to the stables. It gave her better cover, helping her get ever closer. She was stealthily getting herself into position when George's deafening alarm call startled her. She panicked and had to pounce, ready or not. She landed awkwardly in front of one of the fledglings she had an eye on. The poor thing didn't have a chance under those big claws which landed on its chest and crushed it. George was going berserk over her head but it made no difference as she headed back to her den with her prize. George settled down on the boundary fence exhausted, he hated that cat.

He was that angry it took him a few minutes to calm down before checking in on the other fledglings who were silently hiding in some dense undergrowth. The good news is, the remaining three grew up to be fine robins, to their dad's credit. Each of them flew off to new lands to find their way in this world. One of them had briefly become a good friend of the girl, who named her Lizzie. She was a wee beauty who loved to pose for the camera. When the time came for Lizzie to go, the girl wished her the best and off she flew, leaving the Blackhills of Tempo to make a life for herself. The girl secretly hoped they would meet again. With Lizzie gone George was unexpectedly overcome with a sense of loneliness and lack of purpose.

When the wains had fledged, Mildred had said her final farewell to him. He was a lone bachelor boy again. Her season for nesting was over, having done what nature had intended. It was so difficult for them to part ways but it was the 'robin way' and had to be. They had shared an extraordinary robin bond that would forever remain in their hearts. Two lone hearts who had met and become one. What a journey they had together but each would go back to their solitary existence until next spring when they would find new mates and have more wains. This was the 'robin way'. George was convinced in himself he could love no other the way he loved Mildred, which was probably true, but he would love again,

as would Mildred. She wanted him to always sing his song, the ‘song of songs’ that captivated and won her heart. A song that would forever echo in her being. He stood alone on their favourite perch and lifted up his voice, softly at first, then louder and yet louder he sang. He sang with all his might. All living things stood still that dawn as his voice rose and echoed over the Blackhills. It wasn’t the end, it was a new beginning!